read ★ about
WILD ANIMALS

Written by Anyon Ellis
Edited by Carol Watson
Illustrated by Bernard Robinson and Wendy Meadway

CARNIVAL

Animals in the Wild

A wild animal is one that lives in its own natural way and is not kept or bred by Man for his own purposes. Unfortunately, as people take over more and more of the wild places of the world, there are fewer habitats (places to live) for wild animals.

Animals, however, are very adaptable. Many of them have learned to live among people or to ignore them. This book is about the mammals which live in western Europe. Most of the animals are truly wild, but some are *feral*. This means they are wild descendants of animals that were once tamed and kept by Man.

The European bison is one of several wild animals that are in danger of extinction.

European bison

Wild boar

A female wild boar feeding her young.

Sizes: Unless otherwise stated, the lengths of animals given in this book are body lengths, and do not include the tail, if any. The size given is the average size.

Mammals

Mammals are animals which give birth to live young, and then feed them on milk. They are called mammals because the milk comes from the female's *mammary* glands; and the word *mamma* comes from the Latin word meaning breast. Mammals have hair, and they are warm-blooded – that is, they convert some of the food they eat into heat, so that their bodies are warm even in cold weather.

Insect Eaters

Hedgehogs, moles and shrews are part of a group of mammals known as insect-eaters. They feed mainly on insects and other small creatures, and they use up their energy very quickly so they have to keep eating all the time. Insect-eaters have very sensitive noses.

Common Hedgehog

The common hedgehog is found everywhere in Europe except Northern Scandinavia. The hairs of its coat are very thick and form short, sharp pines. When they are in danger some hedgehogs roll into a ball and few animals are willing to attack them. Hedgehogs come out out at night and eat many harmful insects as well as slugs, worms and snails. They sleep through the winter. *Length 250mm.*

Common Hedgehog

Mole

A mole spends most of its time underground, so few people ever see one. It is a tube-shaped creature, with large, spade-like front feet which it uses for digging. Moles live in a maze of underground tunnels and the waste soil from these forms a series of mole-hills on the surface. The mole feeds mainly on earthworms and other small creatures. *Length 140mm.*

Common Shrew

This is the most abundant of the shrews in Europe. It is found in every country except Ireland, and perhaps Portugal. It is a very busy little animal, and eats its own body weight of food every day. The common shrew is active day and night, taking several short rest periods. It makes runs through grass and litter on the ground, and nests in any sheltered spot. When two shrews meet they tend to fight. *Length 75mm.*

Mole

Bats

Bats are the only mammals that can fly, though some other species, such as flying squirrels, can glide. They hunt at night for insects such as moths, and find their way in the dark by means of *sonar*. This is a special feature which means they 'bounce' echoes off objects ahead of them and so can discover where they are. Bats sleep during the day, usually hanging upside down. They also hibernate.

Greater horseshoe bat

This gets its name from a growth on the bat's nose which is shaped like a horseshoe. It is found over southern Europe as far north as southern England and South Wales. *Length 60mm.*

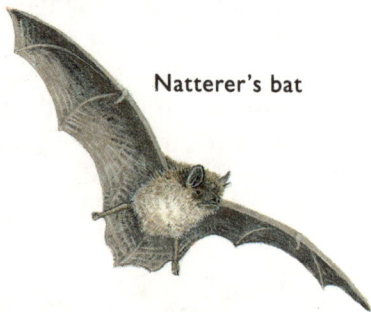

Natterer's bat

Natterer's bat

This lives in most of Europe except the north. It forms huge colonies, usually in trees near water, but often in buildings. During the winter the bats hibernate roosting in small groups or singly, in caves, mines or similar places. They make shrill squeaks which can be clearly heard. *Length 45mm.*

Rabbits and Hares

Rabbit

Rabbits first came from Spain and were introduced by Man into other parts of western Europe. They like to live in grassland, preferably near trees, and dig burrows to live in. The females produce six large litters a year. They feed on grass and other green stuff. *Length 450mm.*

Rabbit

Brown hare

Brown Hare

This lives in open country. It has much larger ears than the rabbit. During the day it lies hidden in a 'form', or nest, which is in tall grass. Hares are solitary animals except in spring, when they rush around in groups or stand up and 'box' with one another. The brown hare is found all over Europe. *Length 650mm.*

Blue hare

The blue, or mountain hare lives in northern Europe and Ireland, and in the Alps. It has shorter ears than the brown hare, and in winter it turns white, (except in Ireland). It is seen more often by day than the brown hare. Some blue hares dig burrows. *Length 550mm.*

Gnawing Animals

Gnawing animals are called rodents and have teeth specially suited to nibbling away at hard material. Most rodents eat plant food, but some such as rats eat anything they can find. Many of them are very small.

Beavers

These are the largest rodents in Europe and live on the banks on slow-flowing rivers and lakes. European beavers live mainly in holes in river banks, but in the north they may build dams to create pools in which they build homes called lodges. The entrances are always underwater. Beavers are brilliant swimmers. The back foot which is used for swimming is much larger than the front foot. *Length 820mm.*

Squirrels

There are about 300 different species of squirrel in the world, but only three are found in western Europe. There are two basic kinds of squirrel: those which live in trees, and those which live on the ground, into which they burrow. They are all active by day.

Red squirrel

The red squirrel is Europe's only native tree squirrel. It eats buds and seeds and in later summer, nuts. The squirrel's reddish-brown coat becomes duller in winter. The squirrel's home is a ball-shaped nest in a tree, called a drey. *Length 250mm.*

Grey squirrel

The grey squirrel came from North America and was introduced into Britain in 1876. It has spread rapidly and replaced the red squirrel in many places. *Length 280mm.*

summer coat

winter coat

spring coat

Red squirrel

Dormice

These are small rodents which look a bit like miniature rats, but behave more like squirrels. Most dormice have bushy tails. They eat buds, fruit and nuts and like squirrels, climb trees to get them. They are active at night, and hibernate for several months.

Common dormouse

This is sometimes called the hazel dormouse and is the smallest of all dormice. It is found in most of Europe except Ireland, Spain, Portugal and the far north. It likes to live among bushes, where it makes a small, ball-shaped nest. Its favourite food is hazelnuts. *Length 75mm.*

Garden dormouse

This is found in most of Europe except the British Isles and Scandinavia. It spends more time on the ground then other dormice, and eats more animal food, such as insects and snails. It makes growling and whistling noises. *Length 140mm.*

Common dormouse

Garden dormouse

Lemmings and Voles

Lemmings and voles live mainly in grasslands, where they make runways through the grass. Lemmings make similar runs through the snow in winter. Their tails are much shorter than mice and they do not hibernate.

Norway Lemming

This lives in Arctic Europe. It is a small, stocky animal that feeds at night on vegetable matter.

About every four years the lemming population increases dramatically, and so there is not enough food to go round. When this happens the lemmings set out on a long migration – and once they start they seem unable to stop. Some try to swim rivers and lakes and are drowned; but a few live to start new colonies. *Length 140mm.*

Common vole

This is found over most of Europe, except Scandinavia and the British Isles. It digs shallow burrows in grassland, and can cause damage to farm pastures. *Length 110mm.*

Common vole

Rats and Mice

There are about 120 species of rat, most of which live in remote areas. Two species, the brown and the black rat haunt places where people live and can do enormous damage and can spread disease.

Mice are closely related to rats, but are much smaller. Mice eat seeds and many other things as well. They have longer snouts and larger ears than voles.

Black rat

Brown rat

Black rat

This is sometimes called the ship rat and is found in southern Europe in seaports and aboard ships. It is the smaller of the two European rats and its colour varies from black to brown. *Length 200mm.*

Brown rat

This is sometimes known as the common rat and is found all over Europe. It is sometimes black, but its ears are always smaller than those of the black rat. *Length 240mm.*

House mouse

This was first introduced to Britain by the Romans and is found wherever there are people. Only a few live in the wild. Apart from the food they eat, house mice do enormous damage and help to spread disease. White mice are a variety of this species. *Length 85mm.*

Wood mouse

Wood mouse

This is sometimes called the Longtailed Field mouse and is found all over Europe except the extreme north. There are more wood mice than any other rodent, but they are rarely seen because they hunt at night. They run, jump and climb easily and are not bothered by severe cold. They store food such as acorns to eat in the winter. *Length 95mm.*

House mouse

Harvest mouse

This is the smallest mouse in Europe and is found nearly everywhere. It makes its home mostly in cereal crops or long grass and is light enough to climb stems in search of seeds. *Length 65mm.*

Flesh-eaters

Animals which eat meat or 'flesh' are called carnivores. They have special teeth adapted for tearing flesh and feed mostly on other animals. They include bears, cats, dogs and weasels.

Bears

Bears are the biggest of the European carnivores. There are two species, the brown bear and the Polar bear and they both have small ears and tiny tails.

Brown bear

The brown bear used to live all over Europe, including Britain, but now they only survive in a few forested, mountainous areas in the Alps, Pyrenees, Scandinavia and eastern Europe. They are not fierce unless provoked and feed on whatever food is available, from fish to honey. *Length 2100mm.*

Brown bear

tracks

Badgers

Weasel Family

The weasel and marten family in Europe consists of about 10 species, with long bodies and short legs. They have musk glands at the base of the tail, with which they can leave scent either to mark a trail or to show the limits of their territory.

Badger

Badgers are like bears in that they use the heel of the foot as well as the sole when walking, but they are in fact members of the weasel family. The badger is a thickset animal, slightly larger than a dachshund, which was the dog bred to hunt badgers by squeezing down the tunnels of their sets. The set is the name given to the badger's home. *Length 700mm.*

Stoat

The stoat is found all over Europe except in countries bordering on the Mediterranean. Stoats living in northern lands turn pure white in winter, except for a black tip to the tail. When this happens they are called ermines. Ermine fur is very valuable. *Length 250mm.*

Weasel

Weasels are the smallest of the carnivores, and are so slim they can pursue voles and mice into their underground tunnels. They are found everywhere in Europe except Ireland. The weasel hunts mainly at night, but may sometimes be seen in the daytime. *Length 220mm.*

European polecat

Polecat

This is larger than the stoat and it leaves a strong and unpleasant scent. The polecat is found over most of Europe except the north; and in the British Isles it lives only in Wales. It is found near water, where it eats frogs and fish as well as almost any other animal it can catch. *Length 360mm.*

Ferret

These are closely related to the polecat and are used to flush out rabbits.

Ferret

Pine marten   Beech marten

Marten

These are cousins to the stoats and although they are larger, are similar in shape. They are about the size of a cat. There are two species. The pine marten has a creamy patch on its throat and chest and lives in forests and climbs trees. The beech marten has a white patch, and hunts mostly on the ground. It does not live in Britain. *Length 450mm.*

Mink

Mink are like large weasels, with dark brown fur which is very valuable. The European mink has a little white on its upper and lower lips and is found mostly in France. The American mink has escaped from fur farms: it has white only on the lower lip, and is found in the British Isles and Scandinavia. Mink live near water and are excellent swimmers. *Length 380mm.*

American mink

European mink

Otter tracks

Otter

Otter

The otter is a large member of the weasel family, with webbed feet which help it to swim. Otters live on the banks of rivers and lakes, and feed on fish and other water animals. They hunt at night. Otters are found all over Europe, but are becoming rare because they have been hunted. *Length 750mm.*

Wolverine

The wolverine lives in the forests of Scandinavia. It looks a bit like a small bear, and eats anything it can find. *Length 750mm.*

Wolverine tracks

Wolverine

The Dog Family

There are four members of the dog family which live wild in western Europe. They all have long legs and are fast runners, which help them when they are hunting.

Wolf

Wolf

The wolf used to roam all over western Europe, but now it is only found in Spain, Italy and Scandinavia. In eastern Europe there are still a great many wolves, and some occasionally migrate westwards. Wolves live in family groups, and work together when hunting large animals such as deer. They bark, growl and wag their tails, just like dogs. They are unpopular because they sometimes kill farm animals. However, they rarely attack people. *Length 1250mm.*

Red fox

Red fox

This is found all over Europe and is a cautious and intelligent animal, which survives constant hunting by man. Some red foxes live on their own, others form family groups. They feed on small animals, their favourites being rabbits and rodents, but they take whatever food they can. Some red foxes live in cities where they raid dustbins and live underneath buildings. They also live on farms and in woods. *Length 770mm.*

Raccoon-dog

This first came from eastern Asia, but has been introduced to Russia because of its fur. Raccoon-dogs are solitary animals, hunting by night and behaving very much like foxes. They have an even wider diet than foxes, eating fruit as well as flesh. *Length 600mm.*

Raccoon-dog

Arctic fox

This animal lives in the frozen wastes of the Arctic Circle, and in the mountains of Norway and Sweden. It has small ears and a grey-brown coat which turns white in the winter. The blue fox is a variety of this animal which stays bluish-grey all the year. Arctic foxes live in small groups, often hunting by daylight. *Length 600mm.*

Arctic foxes

summer coat

winter coat

Cats and Genets

Wild cat

Genet

live in woodlands and eat rodents and birds. *Length 500mm.*

Wild cat

Genet

Although they look a bit like cats, genets are relatives of the mongoose. They first came from Africa, but are now found in Portugal, France and Spain. They

A wild cat looks similar to a large domestic tabbycat. It is to be found in southern and central Europe and in Scotland. Like all cats the wild cat is a solitary animal and likes to hunt at night. *Length 600mm.*

Lynx

There are two species of lynx in Europe. They are larger than domestic cats with tufts on the ears and short tails. The ordinary lynx lives in northern Scandinavia, while a smaller and spottier version, the pardel lynx is found in Spain. They are secretive, solitary animals that hunt by night. *Length: lynx 1100mm; pardel lynx 1000mm.*

Seals

Seals are carnivorous animals that live in coastal waters. Their feet form flippers which are good for swimming but useless on land, so they have to drag themselves around on their bellies when out of water. There are two species to be found off the coast of western Europe. These are the grey and the common seal.

Common seal

pup

Common seal

This is slightly smaller than the grey seal, and is found mostly around the coasts of Scandinavia and the British Isles, sometimes further south in winter. Common seals are generally found lolling on sand banks, where they also breed. *Length 1700mm.*

Grey seal

Grey seals are often found on the rocky parts of the western and northern coasts of the British Isles, and in the Baltic. They breed on small rocky islets, but often land on quiet coasts at low tide. They eat fish. *Length 2600mm.*

Animals with Hoofs

Horses and Ponies

Tarpan

This was the original wild horse of Europe and Asia. It became extinct in 1851, but people have been trying to breed it back, using horses with tarpan blood in them. There is a small herd of tarpans in the Bialowieza Forest of Poland. *Height 1300mm.*

Camargue horse

The Camargue white horse is a breed which has roamed wild since Roman times. They are found in the marshes of the Rhône river delta in France. The colts are born black, and turn white by the age of three. The Camargue horse is squat, with heavy jowls and a bristly coat. Most of these horses are caught and tamed as they get older. *Height 1500mm.*

Camargue horse

Tarpan

Shetland pony

This is the smallest of the semi-wild horses of the British Isles. It stands about 1010mm high at the shoulder, and is very hardy. Until the age of two its coat is like wool, rather than hair, and at all times it is incredibly thick.

New Forest pony

This breed of horse has been roaming the New Forest area of southern England since before the Romans invaded in AD43. In the 19th century it was bred with Arab horses and this has altered the breed and made it less hardy, and less like the original wild pony. *Height 1300mm.*

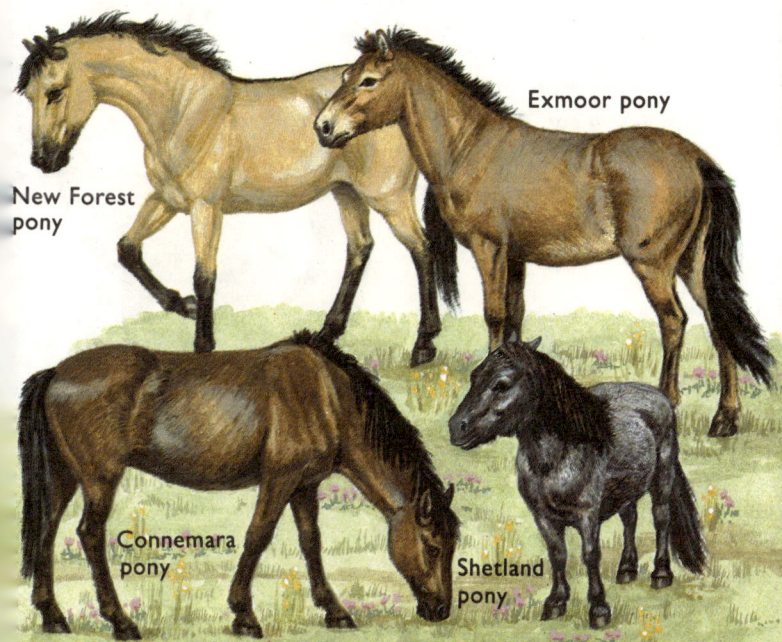

Exmoor pony

New Forest pony

Connemara pony

Shetland pony

Boars, Sheep, Goats and Cattle

Wild boar

Although they are rare, these animals can still be found in dense forests over most of southern and central Europe. The males live all alone, while the females form small groups with their young. They eat anything

Wild boar

they can find, from roots and acorns, to the grub of insects. They even take fish from shallow ponds. *Length 1350mm.*

Ibex

This is the true wild goat. There are two very similar species which live in the Alps and Pyrenees. *Length 1350mm.*

winter coat

Chamois

summer coat

male

female

Mouflon

Feral goat

Alpine Ibex

Robinson

Feral goat

These are wild-living goats which are descended from domesticated breeds. They are different from true wild goats because their horns turn out as well as back. They are the same size and have the same habits as wild goats.

European bison

This animal is sometimes called the wisent, and is related to the North American bison, the 'buffalo' of the Wild West. It was at one time extinct, but herds have now been re-established. Cows and young form herds; males live alone. *Length 2700mm.*

Wild cattle

The wild cattle of Europe were called the aurochs, the last of which died in 1627. Modern cattle are mostly very different but a few ancient breeds still show some of the original features.

Deer

Deer are among Europe's largest wild animals. They graze and chew the cud, like cows. The males of most species have antlers, bony projections from the head, which are shed and regrown every year. While they are growing, the antlers are covered with *velvet*, a smooth covering of skin and short hairs.

Red deer

The red deer is found in isolated places all over Europe. It is – except for the elk – the biggest deer. The hinds (females) and the young form herds, and so do the stags (males). These animals prefer to live on open woodland, but many herds do live on moorland. Red deer feed on grass, young shoots, leaves and acorns. *Length 2000mm.*

hind in
summer coat

DEER TERMS
Buck – Male deer
Doe – Female deer
Fawn – Young deer
Stag or hart – Male red deer
Hind – Female red deer
Calf – Young red deer
Bull – Male elk
Cow – Female elk

stag in
winter coat

Red deer

Sika deer

These are like a small version of the red deer. They come from Japan, and have been introduced into several European countries. Most live in parks, but some live in the wild. During the day they hide in woodland, and come out to feed at dusk. *Length 1200mm.*

Fallow deer

These come from the area around the Mediterranean and are the deer most often kept in parks. They live in large herds, and are active both by day and by night. They behave very much like red deer, only feed more on grass. *Length 1450mm.*

buck

doe

Sika deer

doe

Fallow deer

buck

Roe deer

buck

doe

Roe deer

This is found in most parts of Europe except Ireland and is the smallest of Europe's own deer. It lives in woodlands, feeding by night on the leaves of shrubs and trees. The deer make a sharp barking sound. *Length 1100mm.*

Muntjac

This is a small deer from eastern China. It is not much bigger than a fox, and is the smallest deer now seen in Europe. Muntjacs hide in woodlands, but they give themselves away by their loud, sharp bark. Wild herds of muntjacs are now found in England and France. *Length 800mm.*

Chinese water deer

This also came from China and now lives in wild herds in England and France. Neither males nor females have antlers, but instead the males grow long, slim tusks in their upper jaws. These deer are not seen very often as they feed mostly at night. *Length 900mm.*

Muntjacs

Elk

bull   cow

Reindeer

Elk

The elk is the largest of all the deer. It lives among
the pine forests of Scandinavia and Finland, and is
found all the way round the Arctic Circle. In America it is called a moose. Elks eat the leaves of trees
and water plants, and can dive and swim well. They
tend to lead solitary lives. *Length 2600mm.*

Reindeer

These are the main deer of the far north, mostly living in Lapland. There are a few wild herds, but reindeer are now domesticated. Both females and males
have antlers which is unusual. They also have large
hooves which stop them sinking into the snow. In
winter they feed on lichen. *Length 2000mm.*

Carnival
An imprint of the Children's Division
of the Collins Publishing Group
8 Grafton Street, London WIX 3LA

First published by Granada Publishing 1982.
Published in this abridged edition by Carnival 1989.

ISBN 0-00-194954-3

Printed & bound in Great Britain by
BPCC Paulton Books Limited